spiritual paths
peace

spiritual paths

peace

jay vickers

MQP
MQ Publications Ltd

contents

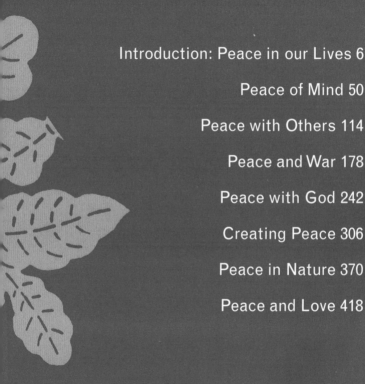

introduction
peace
in our lives

Peace

It is something we all yearn for,
both within ourselves—as peace of
mind, or peace in our hearts—
and in the world around us.

Peace

Like truth, joy, and love,
it is so valuable that it is
beyond any price.

Why, then, is it so elusive? Why do we so seldom feel at peace? Why does there always seem to be so much tension in our lives? And why is it that, somewhere in the world, people are always killing one other?

So how can we
have peace?

How can we
find peace?

How can we
create peace?

In this book we shall look at these ideas, and many more. We will explore peace through the holy writings of different religions, and through the beautiful verse and wise thoughts of great thinkers.

Although you won't find everything there is to know about peace in this book, it will provide inspirational thoughts and challenging ideas.

Each chapter in this book deals with a separate aspect of peace. We start with peace of mind—the importance of being at peace within yourself. Next, we look at being at peace in our dealings with others. Then we step onto the world stage: peace in contrast to war.

The next chapter looks at our relationship with God, and the "peace that passeth understanding," followed by some ideas on how we can create peace. Finally, we look at the peace to be found in the beauty of nature and, closer to home, at peace and love.

This book is designed so that you can read it through from beginning to end, absorb any chapter on its own, or dip in at any point. The quotations are self-contained, so you can dip into it at any point and find a verse or idea that inspires you.

Many of the quotations illustrate or expand upon ideas presented in the text, so when you find one that you particularly like, or that seems helpful, you will probably gain more by reading the pages before and after the quotation.

This book has been written to inspire and comfort you, to help you to understand the nature of peace, and to achieve peace in your life.

Dry your eyes—O dry your eyes,
For I was taught in Paradise
To ease my breast of melodies.

Fairy's Song, John Keats (1795–1821)

Sleep after toil, port after stormy seas, Ease after war, death after life does greatly please.

Edmund Spenser (c. 1552–1599)

When will the world know that peace and propagation are the two most delightful things in it?

Horace Walpole (1717–1797)

But the meek shall inherit the Earth;
and shall delight themselves in the
abundance of peace.

Psalm 37:11

Addressing Himself unto the kings
and rulers of the Earth—may God,
exalted be He, assist them—He
imparted unto them that which
is the cause of the well-being,
the unity, the harmony, and the
reconstruction of the world, and
of the tranquillity of the nations.

Epistle to the Son of the Wolf (Bahá'í scriptures)

Peace is more important than all justice; and peace was not made for the sake of justice, but justice for the sake of peace.

Martin Luther (1483–1546)

When we need peace, sometimes it helps to look around us, to look at the beauty of the world that God created.

Flowers and forests, mountains and streams—there is a wonderful peace to be found in them, whether in simple enjoyment and appreciation, in quiet contemplation, or in active enjoyment of the gifts of nature in our leisure pursuits.

And this our life, exempt from
public haunt,
Finds tongues in trees, books in
the running brooks,
Sermons in stones, and good
in everything.

As You Like It, William Shakespeare (1564–1616)

It was an employment for his idle time, which
was then not idly spent . . . a rest to his mind,
a cheerer of his spirits, a diverter of sadness,
a calmer of unquiet thoughts, a moderator of
passions, a procurer of contentedness; and
that it begat habits of peace and patience in
those that professed and practised it.

Sir Henry Wotton (1568–1639) on angling, quoted in
The Compleat Angler, Izaak Walton (1593–1683)

Through orchard-plots
   with fragrance crowned
The clear cold fountain
   murmuring flows;
And forest leaves with
   rustling sound
Invite to soft repose.

J. H. Merivale (1780–1844)
after Sappho (c. 600 B.C.E.)

And it shall come to pass in that day, that the mountains shall drop down new wine, and the hills shall flow with milk, and all the rivers of Judah shall flow with waters, and a fountain shall come forth of the house of the Lord, and shall water the valley of Shittim.

Joel 3:18

Sadly, humans have a tendency to make war. People fight people, nation fights nation. Despite the merits of the reasons they give for war, peace is driven out. How can we stop this?

It is not enough for us to mouth nice-sounding platitudes. For the world to be at peace, peace must be sought actively. The desire for peace cannot be merely passive.

History is
littered with
the wars which
everybody
knew would
never happen.

Enoch Powell (1912–1998)

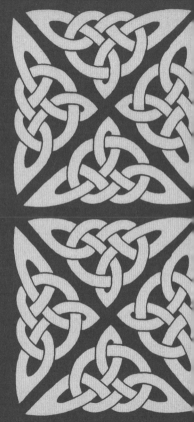

When peace has been broken anywhere, the peace of all countries everywhere is in danger.

Franklin D. Roosevelt (1882–1945)

My object is none other than the betterment of the world and the tranquillity of its peoples. The well-being of mankind, its peace and security, are unattainable unless and until its unity is firmly established. This unity can never be achieved so long as the counsels which the Pen of the Most High hath revealed are suffered to pass unheeded.

Gleanings from the Writings of Bahá'u'lláh (Bahá'í scriptures)

The surest way to peace is through God. It doesn't matter which religion you follow— God is the great unifier. It is only humanity's arrogance and foolishness that divide us.

If we look to God, and take his peace into our hearts, then we will be at peace with our fellow humans. Because if we look to God, we will be at peace within ourselves.

Pass over names and look to qualities,
So that qualities may lead thee
    to essence!
The differences of sects arise from
    His names;
When they pierce to His essence they
    find His peace!

The Spiritual Couplets of Rumi (Sufi writings)

The Lord will give
strength unto his people;
the Lord will bless his
people with peace.

Psalm 29:11

These fires associate with Indra are awake, bringing their light when first the Dawn begins to shine.

May Heaven and Earth, great Pair, observe our holy work. We claim for us this day the favor of the Gods.

Yea, for ourselves we claim the grace of Heaven and Earth, of Saryanavan, of the Hills and Mother Streams.

For innocence we pray to Surya and to Dawn.

So may the flowing Soma bring us bliss today.

May the great Twain, the Mothers, Heaven and Earth, this day preserve us free from sin for peace and happiness.

May Morning sending forth her light drive sin afar. We pray to kindled Agni for felicity.

May this first Dawn bring us the host of gracious Gods: rich, may it richly shine for us who strive for wealth.

The wrath of the malignant may we keep afar. We pray to kindled Agni for felicity.

Rig Veda (Hindu scriptures)

Were men to meditate upon the lives of the Prophets of old, so easily would they come to know and understand the ways of these Prophets that they would cease to be veiled by such deeds and words as are contrary to their own worldly desires, and thus consume every intervening veil with the fire burning in the Bush of divine knowledge, and abide secure upon the throne of peace and certitude.

Kitáb-i-Íqán (Bahá'í scriptures)

The Lord bless thee, and keep thee:
The Lord make His face shine upon
    thee, and be gracious unto thee:
The Lord lift up His countenance upon
    thee, and give thee peace.

Numbers 6:24–26

The Pen of the Divine Expounder exhorteth, at this moment, the manifestations of authority and the sources of power, namely the kings and rulers of the Earth—may God assist them—and enjoineth them to uphold the cause of religion, and to cleave unto it. Religion is, verily, the chief instrument for the establishment of order in the world, and of tranquillity amongst its peoples. The weakening of the pillars of religion hath strengthened the foolish, and emboldened them, and made them more arrogant.

Verily I say: The greater the decline of religion, the more grievous the waywardness of the ungodly. This cannot but lead in the end to chaos and confusion. Hear Me, O men of insight, and be warned, ye who are endued with discernment!

Epistle to the Son of the Wolf (Bahá'í scriptures)

Thy mercy, O Lord, is in the heavens;
and thy faithfulness reacheth unto
the clouds.

Thy righteousness is like the great
mountains; thy judgments are a great
deep: O Lord, thou preservest man
and beast.

How excellent is thy lovingkindness,
O God! therefore the children of men
put their trust under the shadow of
thy wings.

Psalm 36:5–7

Where there is peace, God is.

Proverb

peace
of mind

You cannot have
true peace of mind
if your conscience is troubled.

There is no peace,
saith the Lord,
unto the wicked.

Isaiah 48:22

To gain peace, you must first examine yourself. Are you at ease with yourself? Is your conscience clear? If it is not, then you must deal with whatever it is that is causing you disquiet.

Look into your heart for anger, deceit, bitterness, and unresolved grudges. Look for murderous hatred and petty deceptions. If they are there, then peace will elude you.

Cast out all that is negative within you. Deal with all pain—both your own, and that which you have caused others. And when your conscience is clear, then you will know peace.

From his cradle to his grave
a man never does a single thing which
has any first and foremost object
but one—to secure peace of mind,
spiritual comfort, for himself.

Mark Twain (1835–1910)

Deceit is in the heart of them
that imagine evil: but to the
counselors of peace is joy.

Proverbs 12:20

While you are proclaiming peace with
your lips, be careful to have it even more
fully in your heart.

St. Francis of Assisi (c. 1182–1226)

A peace above all earthly dignities, A still and quiet conscience.

Henry VIII, William Shakespeare (1564–1616)

Although you can always try to improve the conditions of your life, never think that simply by doing so, you will bring yourself peace.

Peace does not depend on having wealth, an easy life, a comfortable job, living in one place and not another, or on being in a relationship—or out of one!

You should seek peace wherever you are, whatever your circumstances. If your peace depends on external conditions, then it is not true peace.

If you have true peace in your heart, you will have peace of mind, and this will remain with you wherever you are and whoever you are with, whether you are rich or poor, healthy or ill, residing in a mansion or living in a tent.

If you are always longing
for a different life,
in order to find peace—

—then you will never find
peace.

They change their clime, not their frame of mind, who rush across the sea. We work hard at doing nothing: we look for happiness in boats and carriage rides. What you are looking for is here, is at Ulubrae, if only peace of mind doesn't desert you.

Horace (65–8 B.C.E.)

If then everything else is common to all that I have mentioned, there remains that which is peculiar to the good man, to be pleased and content with what happens, and with the thread which is spun for him; and not to defile the divinity which is planted in his breast, nor disturb it by a crowd of images, but to preserve it tranquil, following it obediently as a god, neither saying anything contrary to the truth, nor doing anything contrary to justice.

And if all men refuse to believe that he lives a simple, modest, and contented life, he is neither angry with any of them, nor does he deviate from the way which leads to the end of life, to which a man ought to come pure, tranquil, ready to depart, and without any compulsion perfectly reconciled to his lot.

Marcus Aurelius Antoninus (C.E. 121–180)

Shaking off
All longings bred by dreams of fame and gain,
Shutting the doorways of the senses close
With watchful ward; so, step by step, it comes
To gift of peace assured and heart assuaged,
When the mind dwells self-wrapped, and the
    soul broods
Cumberless.
But, as often as the heart
Breaks—wild and wavering—from control, so oft
Let him re-curb it, let him rein it back
To the soul's governance; for perfect bliss
Grows only in the bosom tranquillized,
The spirit passionless, purged from offense,
Vowed to the Infinite.

Bhagavad Gita (Hindu scriptures)

He has cast away Restlessness and Mental Worry; dwelling with mind undisturbed, with heart full of peace, he cleanses his mind from restlessness and mental worry.

The Eightfold Path: Absence of the Five Hindrances
(Buddhist scriptures)

From Canaan Joseph shall return, whose face
A little time was hidden: weep no more—
Oh, weep no more! in sorrow's dwelling-place
The roses yet shall spring from the bare floor!
And heart bowed down beneath a secret pain—
Oh stricken heart! joy shall return again,
Peace to the love-tossed brain—oh, weep no more!

Teachings of Hafiz (Sufi writings)

A padshah was in the same boat with a Persian slave who had never before been at sea and experienced the inconvenience of a vessel. He began to cry and to tremble to such a degree that he could not be pacified by kindness, so that at last the king became displeased as the matter could not be remedied. In that boat there happened to be a philosopher, who said: 'With thy permission I shall quiet him.' The padshah replied: 'It will be a great favor.' The philosopher ordered the slave to be thrown into the water so that he swallowed some of it, whereon he was caught and pulled by his hair to the boat, to the stern of which he clung with both his hands. Then he sat down in a corner and became quiet.

This appeared strange to the king who knew not what wisdom there was in the proceeding and asked for it. The philosopher replied: "Before he had tasted the calamity of being drowned, he knew not the safety of the boat; thus also a man does not appreciate the value of immunity from a misfortune until it has befallen him."

The Gulistan of Sa'di, Sheikh Muslih-Uddin Sa'di Shirazi (c. 1193–1291) (Sufi writings)

To find peace, one must be quiet within. Only in the silence of the soul may peace be found. Contentment is being at peace with yourself. If your heart is pure, and focused only on what is right and good, then you will be at peace.

True contentment comes from pureness of heart, which comes from inner renewal, which itself comes from self-examination.

On the Temple of Apollo at Delphi were the words: Know Thyself. This is the first step to both inner wisdom and inner peace.

Thus the Perfect man
obtains the harmony of his
Heaven-given nature,
and his satisfactions spring up,
he knows not how, as when the
growing grain in spring has been
laid by the rains.

The Writings of Chuang Tzu (Taoist scriptures)

If a Bhikkhu should desire, Brethren, that he should be victorious over discontent and lust, that discontent should never overpower him, that he should master and subdue any discontent that had sprung up within him, let him then fulfill all righteousness, let him be devoted to that quietude of heart which springs from within, let him not drive back the ecstasy of contemplation, let him look through things, let him be much alone!

Kaankheyya-Sutta (If He Should Desire) (Buddhist scriptures)

For nowhere either with more quiet or more freedom from trouble does a man retire than into his own soul, particularly when he has within him such thoughts that by looking into them he is immediately in perfect tranquillity; and I affirm that tranquillity is nothing else than the good ordering of the mind.

Constantly then give to thyself this retreat, and renew thyself; and let thy principles be brief and fundamental, which, as soon as thou shalt recur to them, will be sufficient to cleanse the soul completely, and to send thee back free from all discontent with the things to which thou returnest.

Marcus Aurelius Antoninus (C.E. 121–180)

Or fame or life,
Which do you hold more dear?
Or life or wealth,
To which would you adhere?
Keep life and lose those other things;
Keep them and lose your life—which
   brings
Sorrow and pain more near?

Thus we may see,
Who cleaves to fame
Rejects what is more great;
Who loves large stores
Gives up the richer state.

Who is content
Needs fear no shame.
Who knows to stop
Incurs no blame.
From danger free
Long live shall he.

Tao Te Ching, Lao-tzu
(Taoist scriptures)

And for a disciple thus freed, in whose heart dwells peace, there is nothing to be added to what has been done, and naught more remains for him to do. Just as a rock of one solid mass remains unshaken by the wind, even so, neither forms, nor sounds, nor odors, nor tastes, nor contacts of any kind, neither the desired, nor the undesired, can cause such an one to waver. Steadfast is his mind, gained is deliverance.

And he who has considered all the contrasts on this Earth, and is no more disturbed by anything whatever in the world, the Peaceful One, freed from rage, from sorrow, and from longing, he has passed beyond birth and decay.

The Eightfold Path: The Arahat, or Holy One
(Buddhist scriptures)

Ah, seek the treasure of a mind at rest
And store it in the treasury of Ease;
Not worth a loyal heart, a tranquil breast,
Were all the riches of thy lands and seas!

Ah, scorn, like Hafiz, the delights of earth,
Ask not one grain of favor from the base,
Two hundred sacks of jewels were not worth
Thy soul's disgrace

Teachings of Hafiz (Sufi writings)

I offer with my voice the thoughts well-thought, the words well-spoken, and the deeds well-done, and the heard recital of the Gathas, the Mathras well-composed and well-delivered, and this Lordship, and this Sanctity, and this ritual mastership, and the timely Prayer for blessings, with a complete and sacred offering for the propitiation of the holy Yazads, heavenly and earthly, and for the contentment of the individual soul!

Avesta: Yasna (Zoroastrian scriptures)

Blessed are the pure in heart,
for they shall see God.

Matthew 5:8

For the believer, true inner peace is only to be found through God. Get yourself right with God, and you will be right within yourself.

For the Buddhist or the New Age seeker, the quest is for Enlightenment—for coming to know and to be one with the God Within. This too brings peace.

May the peace of God be with those who have been guided aright through the power of divine guidance.

Selections from the Writings of the Báb
(Bahá'í scriptures)

The words "heal," "healthy," and "hale" (as in "hale and hearty") come from the same root as the word "holy." And "holy" comes from the same root as "whole." If, through God or Enlightenment, your spirit is holy, then your heart is whole, and your inner life is healthy—and you will know that inexpressible deep, inner peace.

Sequestered should he sit,
Steadfastly meditating, solitary,
His thoughts controlled, his passions laid away,
Quit of belongings. In a fair, still spot
Having his fixed abode—not too much raised,
Nor yet too low—let him abide, his goods
A cloth, a deerskin, and the Kusa-grass.

There, setting hard his mind upon The One,
Restraining heart and senses, silent, calm,
Let him accomplish Yoga, and achieve

Pureness of soul, holding immovable
Body and neck and head, his gaze absorbed
Upon his nose-end, rapt from all around,
Tranquil in spirit, free of fear, intent
Upon his Brahmacharya vow, devout,
Musing on Me, lost in the thought of Me.
That Yogin, so devoted, so controlled,
Comes to the peace beyond, My peace, the peace
Of high Nirvana!

Bhagavad Gita (Hindu scriptures)

Peace I leave with you,
my peace I give unto you:
not as the world giveth,
give I unto you.
Let not your heart be
troubled, neither let it
be afraid.

John 14:27

Verily, thy Lord is the All-Knowing. His authority embraceth all things. Rest thou assured in the gracious favor of thy Lord. The eye of His loving-kindness shall everlastingly be directed toward thee. The day is approaching when thy agitation will have been transmuted into peace and quiet calm. Thus hath it been decreed in the Wondrous Book.

Epistle to the Son of the Wolf
(Bahá'í scriptures)

As long as the absolutely true knowledge and insight as regards these Four Noble Truths was not quite clear in me, so long was I not sure, whether I had won that supreme Enlightenment which is unsurpassed in all the world with its heavenly beings, evil spirits, and gods, amongst all the hosts of ascetics and priests, heavenly beings, and men.

But as soon as the absolutely true knowledge and insight as regards these Four Noble Truths

had become perfectly clear in me, there arose in me the assurance that I had won that supreme Enlightenment unsurpassed.

And I discovered that profound truth, so difficult to perceive, difficult to understand, tranquillizing and sublime, which is not to be gained by mere reasoning, and is visible only to the wise.

The Eightfold Path: The Four Noble Truths
(Buddhist scriptures)

But whoso hearkeneth unto me shall dwell safely, and shall be quiet from fear of evil.

Proverbs 1:33

There is one certainty in life, and that is death. It will come to all of us in the end. None can escape it—the rich or the poor, the wise or the foolish, the good man or the bad, the believer or the nonbeliever. And death brings the ultimate peace. In a sense, we have a foretaste of death each night as we sleep, and we know that there is nothing to fear in this. Sleep, too, is a great leveller of men and women, whatever their estate. And sleep, too, brings peace.

Come, Sleep! O Sleep,
the certain knot of peace,

The baiting-place of wit,
the balm of woe,

The poor man's wealth,
the prisoner's release,

Th'indifferent judge between the high
and low

Sir Philip Sidney (1554–1586)

For some, the slowing of life as one ages is in itself a peaceful prospect:

> For mine own part,
> I could be well content
> To entertain the lag-end of my life
> With quiet hours.

Henry IV, Part I,
William Shakespeare (1564–1616)

Some welcome the coming of death, with the peace it will bring:

I shall soon be laid in the quiet grave— thank God for the quiet grave—O! I can feel the cold earth upon me—the daisies growing over me—O for this quiet—it will be my first.

John Keats (1795–1821)

For the believer, death is the fulfillment of hope and faith, and the entry into that final peace.

When the Blessed One died, the venerable Anuruddha, at the moment of his passing away from existence, uttered these stanzas:

"When he who from all craving want was free,
Who to Nirvana's tranquil state had reached,
When the great sage finished his span of life,
No gasping struggle vexed that steadfast heart!

All resolute, and with unshaken mind,
He calmly triumphed o'er the pain of death.
E'en as a bright flame dies away, so was
His last deliverance from the bonds of life!"

Maha-Parinibbana-Sutta (Buddhist scriptures)

May He support us all the day long,
till the shades lengthen,
and the evening comes,
and the busy world is hushed,
and the fever of life is over,
and our work is done!
Then in His mercy
may He give us a safe lodging,
and a holy rest, and peace at the last.

Cardinal Newman (1801–1890)

peace
with others

Sometimes it seems easier to have peace with people we don't know than with those we do. Of those we do know, it can be easier to be at peace with acquaintances rather than with friends, and with friends rather than with family.

The closer it comes to home, the more difficult it can be to achieve peace. Especially within the family, peace between husband and wife, between parents and children, and between brothers and sisters can sometimes seem an impossible dream.

If we cannot achieve peace in our own homes, what hope have we of achieving peace in the world? If charity should begin at home, then so must peace.

Whatever brawls disturb the street,
There should be peace at home.

Love Between Brothers and Sisters, Isaac Watts
(1674–1748)

For there to be peace in our homes, we must first have peace in ourselves. From that will come everything else.

If there is light in the soul,
there will be beauty in
the person.

If there is beauty in the
person, there will be
harmony in the house.

If there is harmony in the
house, there will be order
in the nation.

If there is order in the
nation, there will be peace
in the world.

Chinese proverb

May Hearkening (Sraosha) overcome disobedience within this house, and may peace overcome discord, generosity overcome greed, reverence overcome rebellion, and honesty overcome falsehood.

Khorda Avesta (Zoroastrian scriptures)

He, of a truth, desireth that His servants and His handmaids should be at peace with one another; take heed lest ye do aught that may provoke intransigence amongst you.

Kitáb-i-Aqdas (Bahá'í scriptures)

Charm to secure harmony

Unity of heart, and unity of mind, freedom from hatred, do I procure for you. Do ye take delight in one another, as a cow in her new-born calf!

The son shall be devoted to his father, be of the same mind with his mother; the wife shall speak honeyed, sweet words to her husband!

The brother shall not hate the brother, and the sister not the sister! Harmonious, devoted to the same purpose, speak ye words in kindly spirit!

That charm which causes the gods not to disagree, and not to hate one another, that do we prepare in your house, as a means of agreement for your folk.

Following your leader, of the same mind, do ye not hold yourselves apart! Do ye come here, cooperating, going along the same wagon-pole, speaking agreeably to one another! I render you of the same aim, of the same mind.

Identical shall be your drink, in common shall be your share of food! I yoke you together in the same traces: do ye worship Agni, joining together, as spokes around about the hub!

I render you of the same aim, of the same mind, all paying deference to one person through my harmonizing charm. Like the gods that are guarding the ambrosia, may he (the leader) be well disposed toward you, night and day!

Hymns of the Atharva-Veda (Hindu scriptures)

First keep peace
within yourself,
then you can also
bring peace to others.

Thomas à Kempis (c.1380–1471)

Having secured peace in our own hearts and homes, we can then extend this peace outward to our friends, colleagues, and acquaintances. Like ripples in a pond, peace will spread out from us to touch all those we come into contact with.

Lord, make me an instrument of your
    peace;
where there is hatred, let me sow love;
when there is injury, pardon;
where there is doubt, faith;
where there is despair, hope;
where there is darkness, light;
and where there is sadness, joy.

Grant that I may not so much seek
to be consoled as to console;
to be understood, as to understand,
to be loved as to love;
for it is in giving that we receive,
it is in pardoning that we are pardoned,
and it is in dying to ourselves that we are
   born to eternal life.

St. Francis of Assisi (c. 1182–1226)

For peace to spread, we must project it ourselves. In all our dealings with people, we must be living examples of peace. This is why the Buddha stressed the importance of "right thoughts, right words, and right actions."

This, verily, is the highest, holiest wisdom: to know that all suffering has passed away.

This, verily, is the highest, holiest peace: appeasement of greed, hatred, and delusion.

The Eightfold Path: Nirvana
(Buddhist scriptures)

Blessing and peace, salutation and glory, rest upon Thy loved ones, whom the changes and chances of the world have not deterred from turning unto Thee, and who have given their all, in the hope of obtaining that which is with Thee. Thou art, in truth, the Ever-Forgiving, the All-Bountiful.

Kitáb-i-Aqdas (Bahá'í scriptures)

As we find ourselves at the center of an ever-widening circle of peace, we will gain greater peace ourselves. We will see more and more the beauty and wonder of the humanity of each person that we meet.

Then it was as if I suddenly saw the secret beauty of their hearts, the depths of their hearts where neither sin nor desire nor self-knowledge can reach, the core of their reality, the person that each one is in God's eyes. If only they could see themselves as they really are. If only we could see each other that way all the time, there would be no more war, no more hatred, no more cruelty, no more greed. . . . I suppose the big problem would be that we would fall down and worship each other.

Thomas Merton (1915–1968)

For Mercy has a human heart,
Pity a human face;
And Love, the human form
   divine,
And Peace, the human dress.

William Blake (1757–1827)

Peace is one of the hardest things to achieve, and one of the simplest. In the end, all it comes down to is being a decent human being.

It's a bit embarrassing to have been concerned with the human problem all one's life and find at the end that one has no more to offer by way of advice than "try to be a little kinder."

Aldous Huxley (1894–1963)

Speak not harshly to a man of gentle speech.
Seek not to fight with him who knocks at the
door of peace.

The Gulistan of Sa'di, Sheikh Muslih-Uddin Sa'di Shirazi
(c. 1193–1291) (Sufi writings)

Peace to him that is far off, and to him that is near.

Isaiah 57:19

To him who holds in his hands the Great Image of the invisible Tao, the whole world repairs. Men resort to him, and receive no hurt, but find rest, peace, and the feeling of ease.

Tao Te Ching, Lao-tzu (Taoist scriptures)

Words causing no man woe, words ever true,
Gentle and pleasing words, and those ye say
In murmured reading of a Sacred Writ—
These make the true religiousness of Speech.

Serenity of soul, benignity,
Sway of the silent Spirit, constant stress
To sanctify the Nature—these things make
Good rite, and true religiousness of Mind.

Bhagavad Gita (Hindu scriptures)

Charm to allay discord

Do ye agree, unite yourselves, may your minds be in harmony, just as the gods of old in harmony, sat down to their share!

Same be their counsel, same their assembly, same their aim, in common their thought! The same oblation do I sacrifice for you: do ye enter upon the same plan!

Same be your intention, same your hearts! Same be your mind, so that it may be perfectly in common to you!

Hymns of the Atharva-Veda (Hindu scriptures)

Charm against strife and bloodshed

May we be in harmony with our kinfolk,
in harmony with strangers; do ye,
O Asvins, establish here agreement
among us!

May we agree in mind and thought, may
we not struggle with one another, in a
spirit displeasing to the gods! May not
the din of frequent battle-carnage arise,
may the arrow not fly when the day of
Indra has arrived!

Hymns of the Atharva-Veda (Hindu scriptures)

He avoids tale-bearing, and abstains from it. What he has heard here, he does not repeat there, so as to cause dissension there; and what he heard there, he does not repeat here, so as to cause dissension here. Thus he unites those that are divided; and those that are united, he encourages. Concord gladdens him, he delights and rejoices in concord, and it is concord that he spreads by his words.

He avoids harsh language, and abstains from it. He speaks such words as are gentle, soothing to the ear, loving, going to the heart, courteous and dear, and agreeable to many.

The Eightfold Path: Right Speech (Buddhist scriptures)

Make my heart overflow with love for Thy creatures and grant that I may become the sign of Thy mercy, the token of Thy grace, the promoter of concord amongst Thy loved ones, devoted unto Thee, uttering Thy commemoration, and forgetful of self but ever mindful of what is Thine.

Bahá'í prayer by Abdu'l-Bahá

When thou seest a quarrel be forbearing
Because gentlemen will shut the door of strife.
Use kindness when thou seest contention.
A sharp sword cannot cut soft silk.
By a sweet tongue, grace, and kindliness,
Thou wilt be able to lead an elephant by a hair.

The Gulistan of Sa'di, Sheikh Muslih-Uddin Sa'di Shirazi
(c. 1193–1291) (Sufi writings)

From ourselves, our homes, and our families, to our friends, acquaintances, colleagues, and all those we meet, day by day, week by week, we can bring peace. In this way we can spread peace throughout our entire land, and throughout the world.

Each one of us can be a glowing example, to everyone we encounter, of how the way of peace leads to love and joy. It is the way of happiness, of humanity. It allows us to acknowledge and celebrate the brotherhood and sisterhood of all people.

By spreading peace we can even influence people we have never met. The network of our friends and acquaintances spreads far and wide. Through this network, by example, by word of mouth, even by sending messages of peace by e-mail, peace can grow.

We can influence our politicians. It may be rare that governments, even in democracies, actually do represent the will of their people, but they are certainly conscious of the mood of the people. A sensible government will be guided by that mood. It is up to us to make them see how important peace is to us all.

Thou must show forth that which will ensure the peace and the well-being of the miserable and the down-trodden. Gird up the loins of thine endeavor, that perchance thou mayest release the captive from his chains, and enable him to attain unto true liberty.

Gleanings from the Writings of Bahá'u'lláh (Bahá'í scriptures)

Cromwell, I charge thee, fling away ambition:
By that sin fell the angels; how can man then,
The image of his Maker, hope to win by't?
Love thyself last: cherish those hearts that
    hate thee;
Corruption wins not more than honesty.
Still in thy right hand carry gentle peace,
To silence envious tongues: be just, and fear not.

Henry VIII, William Shakespeare (1564–1616)

The utterance of God is a lamp, whose light is these words: Ye are the fruits of one tree, and the leaves of one branch. Deal ye one with another with the utmost love and harmony, with friendliness and fellowship. He Who is the Daystar of Truth beareth Me witness! So powerful is the light of unity that it can illuminate the whole Earth. The One true God, He Who knoweth all things, Himself testifieth to the truth of these words.

We have, under all circumstances, enjoined on men what is right, and forbidden what is wrong. He Who is the Lord of Being is witness that this Wronged One hath besought from God for His creatures whatever is conducive to unity and harmony, fellowship and concord.

Epistle to the Son of the Wolf (Bahá'í scriptures)

I exhort therefore, that, first of all, supplications, prayers, intercessions, and giving of thanks, be made for all men;

For kings, and for all that are in authority; that we may lead a quiet and peaceable life in all godliness and honesty.

1 Timothy 2:1–2

Her court was pure; her life serene;
God gave her peace; her land reposed;
A thousand claims to reverence closed
In her as Mother, Wife, and Queen

To the Queen, Alfred, Lord Tennyson (1809–1892)

Wherefore, O king, let my counsel
be acceptable unto thee, and break
off thy sins by righteousness, and
thine iniquities by shewing mercy to
the poor; if it may be a lengthening
of thy tranquillity.

Daniel 4:27

The purpose underlying the revelation of every heavenly Book, nay, of every divinely-revealed verse, is to endue all men with righteousness and understanding, so that peace and tranquillity may be firmly established amongst them. Whatsoever instilleth assurance into the hearts of men, whatsoever exalteth their station or promoteth their contentment, is acceptable in the sight of God.

Gleanings from the Writings of Bahá'u'lláh
(Bahá'í scriptures)

Peace is remarkable. It can spread
like dye in water, permeating every place
it touches—yourself, your home and family,
your friends, acquaintances, colleagues, all
those you influence directly or indirectly,
and even your enemies.

You might ask: How can I possibly
show peace toward my enemies? Ask
yourself this instead: Would you like
them to show peace to you?

Whatever is given out, comes back,
be it a blessing or a curse.

Anger breeds anger.
Antagonism breeds antagonism.
Bitterness breeds bitterness.
Hatred breeds hatred.

But peace breeds more peace.

Which is the better choice?

peace

The best way of avenging thyself is not
to become like the wrong doer.

Marcus Aurelius Antoninus (C.E. 121–180)

When a man's ways please the Lord, he maketh even his enemies to be at peace with him.

Proverbs 16:7

The best way to destroy an enemy is to make him a friend.

Abraham Lincoln (1809–1865)

If thou desirest peace from the foe, whenever he
Finds fault behind thy back praise him to his face.
A vicious fellow's mouth must utter words.
If thou desirest not bitter words, sweeten his
   mouth.

The Gulistan of Sa'di, Sheikh Muslih-Uddin Sa'di Shirazi
(c. 1193–1291) (Sufi writings)

This is the Day in which God's most excellent favors have been poured out upon men, the Day in which His most mighty grace hath been infused into all created things. It is incumbent upon all the peoples of the world to reconcile their differences, and, with perfect unity and peace, abide beneath the shadow of the Tree of His care and loving-kindness.

Gleanings from the Writings of Bahá'u'lláh (Bahá'í scriptures)

For he is our peace, who hath made both one, and hath broken down the middle wall of partition between us.

Ephesians 2:14

Ah! When shall all men's good
Be each man's rule, and universal Peace
Lie like a shaft of light across the land?

The Golden Year, Alfred, Lord Tennyson (1809–1892)

Mark the perfect man, and behold the upright: for the end of that man is peace.

Psalm 37:37

Thy loving providence sustains all, Thy protection overshadows all, and the glances of Thy favor are cast upon all. O Lord! Grant Thine infinite bestowals, and let the light of Thy guidance shine.

Illumine the eyes, gladden the hearts with abiding joy. Confer a new spirit upon all people and bestow upon them eternal life. Unlock the gates of true understanding and let the light of faith shine resplendent.

Gather all people beneath the shadow of Thy bounty and cause them to unite in harmony, so that they may become as the rays of one sun, as the waves of one ocean, and as the fruit of one tree. May they drink from the same fountain. May they be refreshed by the same breeze. May they receive illumination from the same source of light.

Thou art the Giver, the Merciful, the Omnipotent.

Bahá'í prayer by Abdu'l-Bahá

God's purpose in sending His Prophets unto men is twofold.

The first is to liberate the children of men from the darkness of ignorance, and guide them to the light of true understanding.

The second is to ensure the peace and tranquillity of mankind, and provide all the means by which they can be established.

Gleanings from the Writings of Bahá'u'lláh (Bahá'í scriptures)

O God, who art the author of peace and lover of concord, in knowledge of whom standeth our eternal life, whose service is perfect freedom; Defend us thy humble servants in all assaults of our enemies.

Book of Common Prayer

O Thou kind Lord! Unite all. Let the religions agree and make the nations one, so that they may see each other as one family and the whole earth as one home. May they all live together in perfect harmony.

Bahá'í prayer by Abdu'l-Bahá

peace

and war

To understand peace, it is necessary to look first at war. Some of the quotations on the next few pages are disturbing, even distressing. They are meant to be.

There is no prettiness in war.
In order to appreciate more the
value of peace, we need to open
our eyes to the horrors of war.

 Not to do so is
to dishonor the
millions of people
who have fought
and died, for
thousands of years,
in hundreds of
lands, and for many
different causes.

In wars, soldiers have died, civilians have died. All were people, individuals, loved by their parents, their husbands and wives, their brothers and sisters, their children. They were people, just like you and me.

It is for them—for their memory, and in the hope that no more will die, that sense will prevail, that war will be defeated by peace—that we look first at the horror and futility of war.

I have many times asked myself
whether there can be more potent
advocates of peace upon earth
through the years to come than
this massed multitude of silent
witnesses to the desolation of war.

George V (1865–1936)

I do wish people would not deceive themselves by talk of a just war. There is no such thing as a just war. What we are doing is casting out Satan by Satan.

Charles Hamilton Sorley (1895–1915)

In war, whichever side may call itself the victor, there are no winners, but all are losers.

Neville Chamberlain (1869–1940)

What difference does it make to the dead, the orphans, and the homeless, whether the mad destruction is wrought under the name of totalitarianism or the holy name of liberty or democracy?

Mahatma Gandhi (1869–1948)

One to destroy, is murder by the law;
And gibbets keep the lifted hand in awe;
To murder thousands, takes a specious name,
"War's glorious art," and gives immortal fame.

Edward Young (1683–1765)

For I must go where lazy Peace
Will hide her drowsy head;
And, for the sport of kings, increase
The number of the dead.

Sir William Davenant (1606–1668)

"Peace upon earth!" was said. We sing it,
And pay a million priests to bring it.
After two thousand years of mass
We've got as far as poison-gas.

Thomas Hardy (1840–1928)

I have seen war. I have seen war on land and sea. I have seen blood running from the wounded. I have seen men coughing out their gassed lungs. I have seen the dead in the mud. I have seen cities destroyed. I have seen 200 limping, exhausted men come out of line—the survivors of a regiment of 1,000 that went forward 48 hours before. I have seen children starving. I have seen the agony of mothers and wives. I hate war.

Franklin D. Roosevelt (1882–1945)

Enough of blood and tears.
Enough.

Yitzhak Rabin (1922–1995)

In war, civilian children starve to death or are mutilated by landmines. But the soldiers who fight and die on the battlefields are often little more than children themselves.

Waste of Blood, and waste of Tears,
Waste of youth's most precious years,
Waste of ways the saints have trod,
Waste of Glory, waste of God,
War!

G. A. Studdert Kennedy (1883–1929)

Older men declare war. But it is
youth who must fight and die.

Herbert Hoover (1874–1964)

Mankind must put an end to war, or war will put an end to mankind.... War will exist until that distant day when the conscientious objector enjoys the same reputation and prestige that the warrior does today.

John F. Kennedy (1917–1963)

Einstein was asked to prophesy what weapons could be used in the Third World War. I am told he replied to the following effect:

"On the assumption that a Third World War must escalate to nuclear destruction, I can tell you what the Fourth World War will be fought with—bows and arrows."

Earl Mountbatten of Burma (1900–1979)

The arms race can kill, though the weapons themselves may never be used . . . by their cost alone, armaments kill the poor by causing them to starve.

Vatican statement to the UN, 1976

The horrors of war—the cost in human lives among other things—should cause us all to rise up and demand peace. If we don't, who will?

When we, the Workers, all demand:
"What are we fighting for?" . . .
Then, then we'll end that stupid
Crime, that devil's madness—War.

Robert W. Service (1874–1958)

The work, my friend, is peace. More than an end to war, we want an end to the beginning of all wars—yes, an end to this brutal, inhuman, and thoroughly impractical method of settling the differences between governments.

Franklin D. Roosevelt (1882–1945)

I hope . . . that mankind will at length, as they call themselves reasonable creatures, have reason and sense enough to settle their differences without cutting throats; for in my opinion there never was a good war, or a bad peace.

Benjamin Franklin (1706–1790)

We have many means of fighting war. Peace demonstrations were popular in the 1960s, and can still be effective in raising publicity and heightening public awareness. They encourage others to join the fight for peace, and tell politicians that you want them to find a solution other than war.

And today we have the Internet. What better than to use it to campaign for peace?

Most religions speak up for peace. As spirituality becomes more personal and we search for our own inner core of peace, we should not forget to look to the ancient religions for inspiration. The fight for peace is nothing new— and goodness and holiness are at the heart of peace.

Violence must be put down! Against cruelty make a stand, ye who would make sure of the reward of Good Thought through Right, to whose company the holy man belongs. His dwelling place shall be in thy House, O Ahura.

Avesta: Yasna (Zoroastrian scriptures)

Let war yield to peace, laurels to paeans.

Cicero (106–43 B.C.E.)

Since wars begin in the minds of men, it is in the minds of men that the defenses of peace must be constructed.

Constitution of UNESCO

With peace in my heart
I do believe
We shall overcome some day

Anonymous

I ain't gonna study war no more
Ain't gonna study war no more
I ain't gonna study war no more

Anonymous

Give peace in our time, O Lord.

Book of Common Prayer

We exhorted all men, and particularly this people, through Our wise counsels and loving admonitions, and forbade them to engage in sedition, quarrels, disputes and conflict. As a result of this, and by the grace of God, waywardness and folly were changed into piety and understanding, and weapons converted into instruments of peace.

Epistle to the Son of the Wolf
(Bahá'í scriptures)

Making peace is not easy—for governments, for the military, for ourselves. It requires effort, and dedication, and often sacrifice. Peace, too, costs—it costs our commitment.

But surely the price is worth paying.

Peace is not only better than war, but infinitely more arduous.

George Bernard Shaw (1856–1950)

Making peace is harder than making war.

Adlai Stevenson (1900–1965)

If peace cannot be maintained with honor, it is no longer peace.

Lord John Russell (1792–1878)

The peace that we seek . . . is one that reflects the lessons of our terrible century: that peace is not true or lasting if it is bought at any cost; that only peace with justice can honor the victims of war and violence; and that, without democracy, tolerance and human rights for all, no peace is truly safe.

Kofi Annan (1999)

How can we make peace? How do we put peace into action? The first thing we can do is to make sure our voices are heard—to cry out for peace! And then we must work for it continuously.

And again I say unto you, sue for peace, not only to the people that have smitten you, but also to all people;

And lift up an ensign of peace, and make a proclamation of peace unto the ends of the Earth;

And make proposals for peace unto those who have smitten you, according to the voice of the Spirit which is in you, and all things shall work together for your good.

Doctrine and Covenants 105:38–40
(Mormon scriptures)

Peace is a daily, a weekly, a monthly process, gradually changing opinions, slowly eroding old barriers, quietly building new structures.

John F. Kennedy (1917–1963)

You can't separate peace from freedom because no one can be at peace unless he has his freedom.

Malcolm X (1925–1965)

Peace cannot be achieved through violence, it can only be attained through understanding.

Albert Einstein (1879–1955)

The Great Being, wishing to reveal the prerequisites of the peace and tranquillity of the world and the advancement of its peoples, hath written:

The time must come when the imperative necessity for the holding of a vast, an all-embracing assemblage of men will be universally realized. The rulers and kings of the Earth must needs attend it, and, participating in its deliberations, must consider such ways and means as will lay the foundations of the world's Great Peace amongst men. Such a peace demandeth that the Great Powers should resolve, for the sake of the tranquillity of the peoples of the Earth, to be fully reconciled among themselves.

Should any king take up arms against another, all should unitedly arise and prevent him. If this be done, the nations of the world will no longer require any armaments, except for the purpose of preserving the security of their realms and of maintaining internal order within their territories. This will ensure the peace and composure of every people, government and nation. We fain would hope that the kings and rulers of the Earth, the mirrors of the gracious and almighty name of God, may attain unto this station, and shield mankind from the onslaught of tyranny.

Gleanings from the Writings of Bahá'u'lláh (Bahá'í scriptures)

I am not only a pacifist but a militant pacifist. I am willing to fight for peace. Nothing will end war unless the people themselves refuse to go to war.

Albert Einstein (1879–1955)

Nonviolence is the first article of my faith. It is also the last article of my creed.

Mahatma Gandhi (1869–1948)

When will our consciences grow so tender that we will act to prevent human misery rather than avenge it?

Eleanor Roosevelt (1884–1962)

Observe good faith and justice toward all nations. Cultivate peace and harmony with all.

George Washington (1732–1799)

With malice toward none; with charity for all; with firmness in the right, as God gives us to see the right, let us strive on to finish the work we are in: to bind up the nation's wounds; to care for him who shall have borne the battle, and for his widow and his orphan, to do all which may achieve and cherish a just and lasting peace among ourselves, and with all nations.

Abraham Lincoln (1809–1865)

They shall beat their swords into plowshares, and their spears into pruning hooks; nation shall not lift up sword against nation, neither shall they learn war any more.

Isaiah 2:4

Nation shall speak peace unto nation.

Motto of the BBC,
Montague John Rendall (1862–1950)

There is no way to peace.
Peace is the way.

A. J. Muste (1885–1967)

I like to believe that people in the long run are going to do more to promote peace than governments. Indeed, I think that people want peace so much that one of these days governments had better get out of their way and let them have it.

Dwight D. Eisenhower (1890–1969)

We may never be strong enough to be entirely nonviolent in thought, word, and deed. But we must keep nonviolence as our goal and make strong progress toward it. The attainment of freedom, whether for a person, a nation, or a world, must be in exact proportion to the attainment of nonviolence for each.

Mahatma Gandhi (1869–1948)

Peace comes from love, freedom, justice, honesty, fairness, and goodwill. If we have these in our hearts, then peace will also be there, and will flow through us to others.

Nonviolence means avoiding not only external physical violence but also internal violence of spirit. You not only refuse to shoot a man, but you refuse to hate him.

Martin Luther King Jr. (1929–1968)

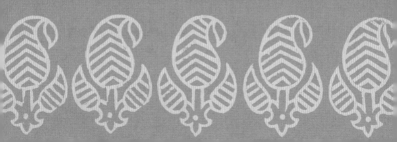

At the center of nonviolence stands the principle of love.

Martin Luther King Jr. (1929–1968)

For he who is a just king knows everything,
And is safe from harm and his mind is at peace.
Justice is the guardian of his steps,
Not guards with drums round his palace.

The Spiritual Couplets of Rumi (Sufi writings)

Instead of loving what you think is peace, love other men and women and love God above all else. Instead of hating all the people you think are warmongers, hate the appetites and disorders in your own soul which are the causes of war.

Thomas Merton (1915–1968)

A good end cannot sanctify evil means; nor must we ever do evil, that good may come of it. . . . It is as great presumption to send our passions upon God's errands, as to palliate them with God's name. . . . We are too ready to retaliate, rather than forgive, or gain by love and information. And yet we could hurt no man that we believe loves us. Let us try then what Love will do: for if men did once see we love them, we should soon find they would not harm us. Force may subdue, but Love gains: and he that forgives first, wins the laurel.

William Penn (1644–1718)

When the power of love
overcomes the love of power
the world will know peace.

Jimi Hendrix (1942–1970)

Every act of love is a work of
peace, no matter how small.

Mother Teresa (1910–1997)

Divine one, give my words
Immortal charm. Lull to a timely rest
O'er sea and land the savage works of war,
For thou alone hast power with public peace
To aid mortality; since he who rules
The savage works of battle, puissant Mars,
How often to thy bosom flings his strength
O'ermastered by the eternal wound of love—
And there, with eyes and full throat backward
    thrown,
Gazing, my Goddess, open-mouthed at thee,
Pastures on love his greedy sight, his breath
Hanging upon thy lips. Him thus reclined
Fill with thy holy body, round, above!
Pour from those lips soft syllables to win
Peace for the Romans, glorious Lady, peace!

Titus Lucretius Carus (c. 99–55 B.C.E.)

We do not have the strength to bring peace to the world on our own. But with God's help, we can begin to work toward peace. And if we are working toward peace, we are doing God's will, whether we are individuals or organizations, religions or governments.

We pray God—exalted be His glory—
and cherish the hope that He may
graciously assist the manifestations
of affluence and power and the
daysprings of sovereignty and glory,
the kings of the Earth—may God aid
them through His strengthening
grace—to establish the Lesser Peace.
This, indeed, is the greatest means for
insuring the tranquillity of the nations.

It is incumbent upon the Sovereigns of the world— may God assist them—unitedly to hold fast unto this Peace, which is the chief instrument for the protection of all mankind. It is Our hope that they will arise to achieve what will be conducive to the well-being of man.

Epistle to the Son of the Wolf
(Bahá'í scriptures)

But if they incline to peace,
incline thou to it too, and rely
upon God; verily, He both hears
and knows.

The Koran 8:61 (Islamic scripture)

The world is in great turmoil, and what is most pathetic is that it has learned to keep away from God, Who alone can save it and alleviate its sufferings. It is our duty, we who have been trusted with the task of applying the divine remedy given by Bahá'u'lláh, to concentrate our attention upon the consummation of this task, and not rest until the peace foretold by the Prophets of God is permanently established . . .

Shoghi Effendi (1897–1957), Bahá'í leader

**Where there is peace,
there is God.**

He who would assist a lord of men in
harmony with the Tao will
not assert his mastery in the kingdom by
force of arms. Such a course
is sure to meet with its proper return.

Tao Te Ching, Lao-tzu (Taoist scriptures)

O ye rulers of the Earth! Wherefore have ye clouded the radiance of the Sun, and caused it to cease from shining? Hearken unto the counsel given you by the Pen of the Most High, that haply both ye and the poor may attain unto tranquillity and peace.

We beseech God to assist the kings of the Earth to establish peace on earth. He, verily, doth what He willeth.

Gleanings from the Writings of Bahá'u'lláh (Bahá'í scriptures)

We supplicate all rulers not to remain deaf to the cry of mankind. Let them do everything in their power to save peace. By so doing they will spare the world the horrors of a war that would have disastrous consequences, such as nobody can foresee.

Pope John XXIII (1881–1963)

Blessed are the peacemakers,
for they shall be called the
children of God.

Matthew 5:9

peace

with God

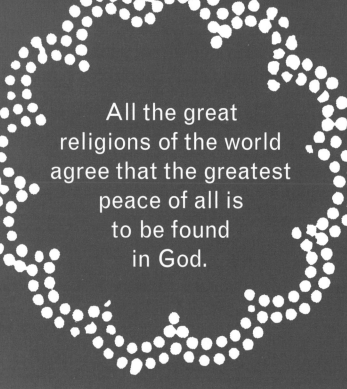

All the great
religions of the world
agree that the greatest
peace of all is
to be found
in God.

In the Religions of the Book, God's peace is found in different ways. In Judaism, it is through knowledge of God's law, and following that law. In Christianity, it comes through God's grace. In Islam, peace is found through submission to God's will. In the Bahá'í faith, peace comes through the unity of all peoples under God.

In Hinduism and Buddhism,
peace comes in renouncing the
world; but the greatest peace
of all comes through stepping off
the endless wheel of existence,
into nirvana.

Other religions lead to peace in
different ways, but all agree:

Peace in God brings
rest and security,
trust and joy.

The peace of God,
which passeth all understanding,
shall keep your hearts and
minds through Christ Jesus.

Philippians 4:7

This, truly, is the Peace, this is the Highest, namely the end of all formations, the forsaking of every substratum of rebirth, the fading away of craving: detachment, extinction—Nirvana.

The Eightfold Path: Nirvana (Buddhist scriptures)

O my brother! Take thou the step of the spirit, so that, swift as the twinkling of an eye, thou mayest flash through the wilds of remoteness and bereavement, attain the Ridvan of everlasting reunion, and in one breath commune with the heavenly Spirits. For with human feet thou canst never hope to traverse these immeasurable distances, nor attain thy goal. Peace be upon him whom the light of truth guideth unto all truth, and who, in the name of God, standeth in the path of His Cause, upon the shore of true understanding.

Kitáb-i-Íqán (Bahá'í scriptures)

For the believer, the peace of God is both present and future, now and in the hereafter.

The future world can only be a promise, but to know the peace of God in one's heart now, today, is the greatest blessing.

With peace in one's heart comes a sense of security, of refuge, of rightness with God, and through God, with our fellow human beings. The peace of God permeates every moment of a believer's life.

And I will make with them a covenant of peace, and will cause the evil beasts to cease out of the land: and they shall dwell safely in the wilderness, and sleep in the woods.

Ezekiel 34:25

Richer than holy fruit on Vedas growing,
Greater than gifts, better than prayer or fast,
Such wisdom is! The Yogi, this way knowing,
Comes to the Utmost Perfect Peace at last.

Bhagavad Gita (Hindu scriptures)

Reflect: Who in this world is able to manifest such transcendent power, such pervading influence? All these stainless hearts and sanctified souls have, with absolute resignation, responded to the summons of His decree. Instead of complaining, they rendered thanks unto God, and amidst the darkness of their anguish they revealed naught but radiant acquiescence to His will.

Kitáb-i-Íqán (Bahá'í scriptures)

To give light unto them that sit in darkness and in the shadow of death, to guide our feet into the way of peace.

Luke 1:79

Rest thou assured in the gracious favor of thy Lord. The eye of His loving-kindness shall everlastingly be directed toward thee. The day is approaching when thy agitation will have been transmuted into peace and quiet calm. Thus hath it been decreed in the wondrous Book.

Kitáb-i-Aqdas
(Bahá'í scriptures)

And his heart becomes free from sensual
passion, free from the passion for existence,
free from the passion of ignorance. "Freed
am I!"—this knowledge arises in the
liberated one; and he knows:
"Exhaused is rebirth, fulfilled the Holy Life;
what was to be done, has been done; naught
remains more for this world to do."
Forever am I liberated
   this is the last time that I'm born,
No new existence waits for me.

The Eightfold Path: Nirvana
(Buddhist scriptures)

To Varuna and Mitra we offer with
    songs, as Atri did.
Sit on the sacred grass to drink the
    Soma juice.
By Ordinance and Law ye dwell in
    peace secure, bestirring men.
Sit on the sacred grass to drink the
    Soma juice.
May Varuna and Mitra, for our help,
    accept the sacrifice.
Sit on the sacred grass to drink the
    Soma juice.

Rig Veda (Hindu scriptures)

Far from the glory of God, the Lord of heaven and earth, the Lord of creation, be that which is affirmed of Him by the peoples of the world, except by such as faithfully observe His precepts. May the peace of God rest upon the sincere among His servants.

Selections from the Writings of the Báb
(Bahá'í scriptures)

Now the God of hope fill you with all joy and peace in believing, that ye may abound in hope, through the power of the Holy Ghost.

Romans 15:13

In His will
is our peace.

Paradiso, Dante (1265–1321)

Grant, we beseech thee, merciful Lord, to thy faithful people pardon and peace, that they may be cleansed from all their sins, and serve thee with a quiet mind.

Book of Common Prayer

Most gracious God, who brings to life and lulls to rest, he who controls the world, what moves not and what moves, May he vouchsafe us shelter—Savitar the God—for tranquil life, with triple bar against distress.

Rig Veda (Hindu scriptures)

Come, Holy Ghost, our souls inspire,
And lighten with celestial fire.
Thou the anointing Spirit art,
Who dost thy seven-fold gifts impart.

Thy blessed unction from above,
Is comfort, life, and fire of love.
Enable with perpetual light
The dullness of our blinded sight.

Anoint and cheer our soiled face
With the abundance of thy grace.
Keep far our foes, give peace at home:
Where thou art guide, no ill can come.

Veni Creator Spiritus, trans. John Cosin (1594–1672),
Book of Common Prayer

Therefore, O brother! kindle with the oil of wisdom the lamp of the spirit within the innermost chamber of thy heart, and guard it with the globe of understanding, that the breath of the infidel may extinguish not its flame nor dim its brightness.

Thus have We illuminated the heavens of utterance with the splendors of the Sun of divine wisdom and understanding, that thy heart may find peace, that thou mayest be of those who, on the wings of certitude, have soared unto the heaven of the love of their Lord, the All-Merciful.

Kitáb-i-Íqán (Bahá'í scriptures)

For the kingdom of God
is not meat and drink;
but righteousness, and
peace, and joy in the
Holy Ghost.

Romans 14:17

But learn that he who doeth the works of righteousness shall receive his reward, even peace in this world, and eternal life in the world to come.

Doctrine and Covenants 59:23
(Mormon scriptures)

The Lord shall give strength
  unto his people:
The Lord shall give his people
  the blessing of peace

Psalm 29:10, *Book of Common Prayer*

For them is an abode of peace; and their Lord, He is their patron for what they have done.

The Koran 6:127 (Islamic scripture)

Peace be upon them that beseech forgiveness from God thy Lord, saying: "Verily, praise be unto God, the Lord of the worlds."

Selections from the Writings of the Báb
(Bahá'í scriptures)

And suddenly
there was with the
angel a multitude
of the heavenly
host praising God,
and saying,

Glory to God in
the highest, and on
earth peace, good
will toward men.

Luke 2:13–14

And behold, the Holy Spirit of God did come down from heaven, and did enter into their hearts, and they were filled as if with fire, and they could speak forth marvelous words.

And it came to pass that there came a voice unto them, yea, a pleasant voice, as if it were a whisper, saying:

Peace, peace be unto you, because of your faith in my Well Beloved, who was from the foundation of the world.

Helaman 5:45–47, Book of Mormon

Blessed is the one who discovereth the fragrance of inner meanings from the traces of this Pen through whose movement the breezes of God are wafted over the entire creation, and through whose stillness the very essence of tranquillity appeareth in the realm of being.

Glorified be the All-Merciful,
the Revealer of so inestimable
a bounty. Say: Because He
bore injustice, justice hath
appeared on earth, and
because He accepted
abasement, the majesty
of God hath shone forth
amidst mankind.

The Kitáb-i-Aqdas (Bahá'í scriptures)

Yea! knowing Me the source of all, by Me
    all creatures wrought,
The wise in spirit cleave to Me, into My
    Being brought;
Hearts fixed on Me; breaths breathed to
    Me; praising Me, each to each,
So have they happiness and peace, with
    pious thought and speech;

And unto these—thus serving well, thus
    loving ceaselessly—
I give a mind of perfect mood, whereby
    they draw to Me;
And, all for love of them, within their
    darkened souls I dwell,
And, with bright rays of wisdom's lamp,
    their ignorance dispel.

Bhagavad Gita (Hindu scriptures)

For the mountains shall depart and the hills be removed, but my kindness shall not depart from thee, neither shall the covenant of my peace be removed, saith the Lord that hath mercy on thee.

O thou afflicted, tossed with tempest, and not comforted! Behold, I will lay thy stones with fair colors, and lay thy foundations with sapphires.

And I will make thy windows of agates, and thy gates of carbuncles, and all thy borders of pleasant stones.

And all thy children shall be
taught of the Lord; and great shall
be the peace of thy children.

In righteousness shalt thou be established; thou
shalt be far from oppression for thou shalt not fear,
and from terror for it shall not come near thee.

3 Nephi 22:10–14, *Book of Mormon*

Or let him take hold of my strength, that he may make peace with me; and he shall make peace with me.

Isaiah 27:5

O God, from whom all holy desires, all good counsels, and all just works do proceed,
Give unto thy servants that peace which the world cannot give.

Book of Common Prayer

Send down upon them that which will bring comfort to their minds, will rejoice their inner beings, will impart assurance to their hearts and tranquillity to their bodies, and will enable their souls to ascend to the presence of God, the Most Exalted, and to attain the supreme Paradise and such retreats of glory as Thou hast destined for men of true knowledge and virtue.

Selections from the Writings of the Báb
(Bahá'í scriptures)

Peace I leave with you, my peace I give unto you: not as the world giveth, give I unto you. Let not your heart be troubled, neither let it be afraid.

John 14:27

Verily I am Thy servant, O my God, and Thy poor one and Thy suppliant and Thy wretched creature. I have arrived at Thy gate, seeking Thy shelter. I have found no contentment save in Thy love, no exultation except in Thy remembrance, no eagerness but in obedience to Thee, no joy save in Thy nearness, and no tranquillity except in reunion with Thee, notwithstanding that I am conscious that all created things are debarred from Thy sublime Essence and the entire creation is denied access to Thine inmost Being.

Selections from the Writings of the Báb
(Bahá'í scriptures)

We are entirely unworthy to be accepted into God's presence, but if we confess our faults and failings, and come to Him in humility and thankfulness, He will draw us to Him and grant us His peace. This is the miracle of God's peace.

Now the Lord of peace himself give you peace always by all means.
The Lord be with you all.

2 Thessalonians 3:16

It is inconceivable that the One Creator God—the God of love and peace—would ever turn His face away from us. If we ask for His peace, He will surely give it to us.

In many religions, the greatest peace of all, for a true believer, is the promise of the peace of heaven. No one knows what heaven will be like, but the Scriptures suggest it will be wonderful.

And then shall it come to pass, that the spirits of those who are righteous are received into a state of happiness, which is called paradise, a state of rest, a state of peace, where they shall rest from all their troubles and from all care, and sorrow.

Alma 40:12, *Book of Mormon*

Create in me a pure heart, O my God, and renew a tranquil conscience within me, O my Hope! Through the spirit of power confirm Thou me in Thy Cause, O my Best-Beloved, and by the light of Thy glory reveal unto me Thy path, O Thou the Goal of my desire! Through the power of Thy transcendent might lift me up unto the heaven of Thy holiness, O Source of my being, and by the breezes of Thine eternity gladden me, O Thou Who art my God!

Let Thine everlasting melodies breathe tranquillity on me, O my Companion, and let the riches of Thine ancient countenance deliver me from all except Thee, O my Master, and let the tidings of the revelation of Thine incorruptible Essence bring me joy, O Thou Who art the most manifest of the manifest and the most hidden of the hidden!

Bahá'í prayer by Bahá'u'lláh

But the souls of the righteous are in the hand of God, and there shall no torment touch them.

In the sight of the unwise they seemed to die; and their departure is taken for misery,

And their going from us to be utter destruction: but they are in peace.

For though they be punished in the sight of men, yet is their hope full of immortality.

And having been a little chastised, they shall be greatly rewarded: for God proved them, and found them worthy for himself.

Wisdom of Solomon 3:1–5

The faithful . . . are indeed the inmates of the all-highest Paradise wherein they will abide for ever.

Verily they will see naught therein save that which hath proceeded from God, nothing that will lie beyond the compass of their understanding. There they will meet the believers in Paradise, who will address them with the words "Peace, Peace" lingering on their lips . . .

Selections from the Writings of the Báb
(Bahá'í scriptures)

creating

peace

How do we create peace, first within ourselves and in our own lives, and then around us? Where do we begin?

It might sound old-fashioned, but you can't be at peace within yourself, and you certainly can't be an example of peace to others, if your life is an untidy, unclean, selfish mess.

Not easy 'tis
For one who violates by ugly deeds
The bonds of common peace to pass a life
Composed and tranquil.

Titus Lucretius Carus (c. 99–55 B.C.E.)

To give oneself up to indulgence in sensual pleasure, the base, common, vulgar, unholy, unprofitable; and also to give oneself up to self-mortification, the painful, unholy, unprofitable: both these two extremes the Perfect One has avoided, and found out the Middle Path, which makes one both to see and to know, which leads to peace, to discernment, to enlightenment, to Nirvana.

The Eightfold Path: The Two Extremes and the Middle Path (Buddhist scriptures)

Come, ye children, hearken unto me: I will teach you the fear of the Lord.

What man is he that desireth life, and loveth many days, that he may see good? Keep thy tongue from evil, and thy lips from speaking guile.

Depart from evil, and do good; seek peace, and pursue it.

Psalm 34:11–14

Wilt thou not cease to value many other things too? Then thou wilt be neither free, nor sufficient for thy own happiness, nor without passion. For of necessity thou must be envious, jealous, and suspicious of those who can take away those things, and plot against those who have that which is valued by thee. Of necessity a man must be altogether in a state of perturbation who wants any of these things; and besides, he must often find fault with the gods.

But to reverence and honor thy own mind will make thee content with thyself, and in harmony with society, and in agreement with the gods, that is, praising all that they give and have ordered.

Marcus Aurelius Antoninus (C.E. 121–180)

If we want peace in our lives, we need to put wrong living away from us, and embrace right living. It is no coincidence that the words "peace" and "righteousness" occur together so often in the Bible.

Righteousness should not mean a stuffy, pompous life. Pretending to be righteous is hypocritical, but living a truly righteous life means being just and honorable, doing what is right, and being an upright, decent person.

Living this life brings peace within, and lets peace shine out to others.

And the work of righteousness shall be peace; and the effect of righteousness quietness and assurance for ever.

And my people shall dwell in a peaceable habitation, and in sure dwellings, and in quiet resting places.

Isaiah 32:17–18

Great peace have they which love thy law: and nothing shall offend them.

Psalm 119:165

Mercy and truth are met together: righteousness and peace have kissed each other. Truth shall flourish out of the Earth: and righteousness hath looked down from heaven.

Psalm 85:10–11, Book of Common Prayer

We entreat God to deliver the light of equity and the sun of justice from the thick clouds of waywardness, and cause them to shine forth upon men. No light can compare with the light of justice. The establishment of order in the world and the tranquillity of the nations depend upon it.

Epistle to the Son of the Wolf
(Bahá'í scriptures)

Be perfect, be of good comfort, be of one mind, live in peace; and the God of love and peace shall be with you.

2 Corinthians 13:11

To regard benevolence as the source of all kindness, righteousness as the source of all distinctions, propriety as the rule of all conduct, and music as the idea of all harmony, thus diffusing a fragrance of gentleness and goodness, constitutes what we call the Superior man.

The Writings of Chuang Tzu
(Taoist scriptures)

The meek-spirited shall
possess the Earth: and
shall be refreshed in the
multitude of peace.

Psalm 37:11, Book of Common Prayer

Keep innocency, and take heed
    unto the thing that is right:
For that shall bring a man peace
    at the last.

Psalm 37:38, *Book of Common Prayer*

Living a life of righteousness
or perfection, is not easy.
It takes effort and dedication,
and it means devoting yourself to
doing good, not just in the eyes of
man, but in the sight of God.

It may be a struggle at times to live a just and righteous life. To others it may seem hard work, toil, labor. But the man or woman who lives such a life, lovingly and joyfully, paradoxically finds that their work is not drudgery, but the path to peace.

Whoso performeth—diligent, content—
The work allotted him, whate'er it be,
Lays hold of perfectness! Hear how a man
Findeth perfection, being so content:
He findeth it through worship—wrought by work—
Of Him that is the Source of all which lives,
Of Him by Whom the universe was stretched.

Bhagavad Gita (Hindu scriptures)

What seems night to you is broad day to me;
What seems a prison to you is a garden to me.
Busiest occupation is rest to me.

The Spiritual Couplets of Rumi (1207–1273) (Sufi writings)

One of the great lessons of the scriptures of the world's religions is that a life of righteousness, which leads to peace, is a life of beautiful simplicity.

Especially in our hectic twenty-first century lives, we pursue complexity all the time. We rush from one thing to another, leaving things half-finished because we must be somewhere else, doing something else. Everything is rushed, complicated, untidy—and dissatisfying.

Stop! Pause, rest, think, learn to be . . .

Whatever you are doing,
focus on that one thing.
Put everything else out of your mind.
Set aside time in your busy life
to devote to simply being.

In this simplicity,
you will find peace.

—

If you keep your body as it should be, and look only at the one thing, the Harmony of Heaven will come to you. Call in your knowledge, and make your measures uniform, and the spiritual will come and lodge with you; the Attributes of the Tao will be your beauty, and the Tao itself will be your dwelling-place. You will have the simple look of a newborn calf, and will not seek to know the cause of your being what you are.

The Writings of Chuang Tzu (Taoist scriptures)

That man alone is wise
Who keeps the mastery of himself! If one
Ponders on objects of the sense, there springs
Attraction; from attraction grows desire,
Desire flames to fierce passion, passion breeds
Recklessness; then the memory—all betrayed—
Lets noble purpose go, and saps the mind,
Till purpose, mind, and man are all undone.

But, if one deals with objects of the sense
Not loving and not hating, making them
Serve his free soul, which rests serenely lord,
Lo! such a man comes to tranquillity;
And out of that tranquillity shall rise
The end and healing of his earthly pains,
Since the will governed sets the soul at peace.
The soul of the ungoverned is not his,
Nor hath he knowledge of himself; which lacked,
How grows serenity? and, wanting that,
Whence shall he hope for happiness?

Bhagavad Gita (Hindu scriptures)

Occupy thyself with few things, says the philosopher, if thou wouldst be tranquil. But consider if it would not be better to say, Do what is necessary, and whatever the reason of the animal which is naturally social requires, and as it requires. For this brings not only the tranquillity which comes from doing well, but also that which comes from doing few things.

For the greatest part of what we say and do being unnecessary, if a man takes this away, he will have more leisure and less uneasiness. Accordingly on every occasion a man should ask himself, Is this one of the unnecessary things? Now a man should take away not only unnecessary acts, but also, unnecessary thoughts, for thus superfluous acts will not follow after.

Marcus Aurelius Antoninus (C.E. 121–180)

Herein, brethren, a Bhikkhu, wisely reflecting, cultivates that part of the higher wisdom called Mindfulness, dependent on seclusion, dependent on passionlessness, dependent on the utter ecstasy of contemplation, resulting in the passing off of thoughtlessness.

He cultivates that part of the higher wisdom called Search after Truth, he cultivates that part of the higher wisdom called Energy, he cultivates that part of the higher wisdom called joy, he cultivates that part of the higher wisdom called Peace, he cultivates that part of the higher wisdom called Earnest Contemplation, he cultivates that part of the higher wisdom called Equanimity—each dependent on seclusion, dependent on passionlessness, dependent on the utter ecstasy of contemplation, resulting in the passing off of thoughtlessness.

Sabbsava-Sutta (Buddhist scriptures)

Ten men eat at a table but two dogs will contend for one piece of carrion. A greedy person will still be hungry with the whole world, whilst a contented man will be satisfied with one bread. Wise men have said that poverty with content is better than wealth and not abundance.

The Gulistan of Sa'di, Sheikh Muslih-Uddin Sa'di Shirazi (c. 1193–1291) (Sufi writings)

Simplicity is not a goal, but one arrives at simplicity in spite of oneself, as one approaches the real meaning of things.

Constantin Brancusi (1876–1957)

Seek the simple life,
the life where, even if you are
working, you can find the space
within yourself to be at rest.

Tranquillity
is being at peace with yourself.

True joy,
true happiness,
come from
living in a deep,
inner peace.

Fair quiet, have I found thee here,
And Innocence thy Sister dear!
Mistaken long, I sought you then
In busie Companies of Men.
Your sacred Plants, if here below,
Only among the Plants will grow
Society is all but rude,
To this delicious Solitude.

The Garden, Andrew Marvell (1621–1678)

And whenever, whilst enraptured in mind, his spiritual frame and his mind become tranquil—at such a time he has gained and is developing the Element of Enlightenment "Tranquillity;" and thus this element of enlightenment reaches fullest perfection.

And whenever, whilst being tranquillized in his spiritual frame and happy, his mind becomes concentrated—at such a time he has gained and is developing the Element of Enlightenment "Concentration;" and thus this element of enlightenment reaches fullest perfection.

The Eightfold Path: Nirvana Through
Watching Over Breathing
(Buddhist scriptures)

Poetry is the spontaneous overflow of powerful feelings: it takes its origin from emotion recollected in tranquillity.

William Wordsworth (1770–1850)

O contentment, make me rich
For besides thee no other wealth exists.
Loqman selected the corner of patience.
Who has no patience has no wisdom.

The Gulistan of Sa'di, Sheikh Muslih-Uddin Sa'di Shirazi
(c. 1193–1291) (Sufi writings)

O Happiness! our being's end and aim!
Good, pleasure, ease, content! whate'er
  they name:
That something still which prompts
  th'eternal sigh,
For which we bear to live, or dare to die.

Alexander Pope (1688–1744)

The sage asked the spirit of wisdom thus: "Which is that good work which is greater and better than all good works, and no trouble whatever is necessary for its performance?"

The spirit of wisdom answered thus: "To be grateful in the world, and to wish happiness for every one. This is greater and better than every good work, and no commotion whatever is necessary for its performance."

Menog-i Khrad (Zoroastrian scriptures)

The deepest peace of all, say the world's religions, comes from being at one with God.

If we have the peace of God in our hearts, then we may experience tranquillity, happiness, joy, love, and the mystery of spiritual peace.

This deep spirituality also causes wonderful changes in our lives. We know peace within ourselves, but others can see this peace in us too.

It is evident that nothing short of this mystic transformation could cause such spirit and behavior, so utterly unlike their previous habits and manners, to be made manifest in the world of being. For their agitation was turned into peace, their doubt into certitude, their timidity into courage. Such is the potency of the Divine Elixir, which, swift as the twinkling of an eye, transmuteth the souls of men!

Kitáb-i-Íqán (Bahá'í scriptures)

But the fruit of the Spirit is love, joy, peace, long-suffering, gentleness, goodness, faith, meekness, temperance: against such there is no law.

Galatians 5:22–23

And these are they who have published peace, who have brought good tidings of good, who have published salvation; and said unto Zion: Thy God reigneth!

And O how beautiful upon the mountains were their feet!

And again, how beautiful upon the mountains are the feet of those that are still publishing peace!

And again, how beautiful upon the mountains are the feet of those who shall hereafter publish peace, yea, from this time henceforth and forever.

And behold, I say unto you, this is not all. For O how beautiful upon the mountains are the feet of him that bringeth good tidings, that is the founder of peace, yea, even the Lord, who has redeemed his people; yea, him who has granted salvation unto his people.

Mosiah, Book of Mormon 15:14–18

Meditate profoundly, that the secret of things unseen may be revealed unto you, that you may inhale the sweetness of a spiritual and imperishable fragrance, and that you may acknowledge the truth that from time immemorial even unto eternity the Almighty hath tried, and will continue to try, His servants, so that light may be distinguished from darkness, truth from falsehood, right from wrong, guidance from error, happiness from misery, and roses from thorns.

Kitáb-i-Íqán (Bahá'í scriptures)

This is the Middle Path which the Perfect One has found out, which makes one both to see and to know, which leads to peace, to discernment, to enlightenment, to Nirvana.

Free from pain and torture is this path, free from groaning and suffering; it is the perfect path.

Truly, like this path there is no other path to the purity of insight. If you follow this path, you will put an end to suffering.

The Eightfold Path (Buddhist scriptures)

Consort with all religions with amity and concord, that they may inhale from you the sweet fragrance of God. Beware lest amidst men the flame of foolish ignorance overpower you. All things proceed from God and unto Him they return. He is the source of all things and in Him all things are ended.

Kitáb-i-Aqdas (Bahá'í scriptures)

And all thy children shall be taught of the Lord; and great shall be the peace of thy children.

Isaiah 54:13

peace
in nature

There is probably nothing more peaceful than sitting on a hillside watching a beautiful sunset. The glory, majesty, and hugeness of nature are transformed into serenity and a feeling of absolute rightness.

Standing on a rocky seashore looking out at the tumbling breakers—a scene of awesome power—somehow conjures up a moment of deep peacefulness.

On a clear night, miles from the city lights, look up at the starry sky. It is simply not possible to grasp in one's mind the distance of each point of light. The world becomes tiny, and you become even tinier.

And yet it is so peaceful.

The grandeur of nature can be awesome, overwhelming.

But the peace that we can experience from nature is incomparable.

Silver of moon and gold
Of sun are glories rolled
From Thy great eyes; Thy visage,
    beaming tender
Throughout the stars and skies,
Doth to warm life surprise
Thy Universe. The worlds are filled
    with wonder

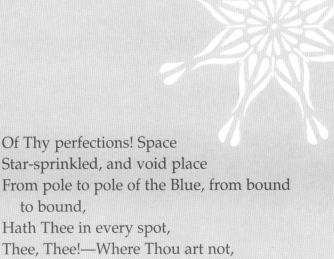

Of Thy perfections! Space
Star-sprinkled, and void place
From pole to pole of the Blue, from bound
   to bound,
Hath Thee in every spot,
Thee, Thee!—Where Thou art not,
O Holy, Marvelous Form! is nowhere found!

Bhagavad Gita (Hindu scriptures)

For ye shall go out with joy,
and be led forth with
peace: the mountains and
the hills shall break forth
before you into singing,
and all the trees of the field
shall clap their hands.

Isaiah 55:12

There is peace in the beauty of trees and flowers—in trees, for the long, slow life in their sap, which flows beneath the rough bark we can feel with our hands—in flowers, for their loveliness, and their impermanence.

In the small town of Glastonbury in southern England, a place of great spirituality, there is a garden at the foot of the hill, Glastonbury Tor. The Chalice Well Garden has only white flowers. Individuals, lovers, families, elderly people, all go there for the peacefulness of the place.

One might expect children to be running around and playing—but no. Even small children respond to the deep spirituality of the garden. They, too, feel its peacefulness, and become quieter and reverential.

I know a bank whereon the wild thyme blows,
Where oxlips and the nodding violet grows
Quite over-canopied with luscious woodbine,
With sweet musk-roses, and with eglantine:
There sleeps Titania some time of the night,
Lull'd in these flowers with dances and delight;
And there the snake throws her enamell'd skin,
Weed wide enough to wrap a fairy in.

A Midsummer Night's Dream,
William Shakespeare (1564–1616)

To see a World in a Grain of Sand,
And a Heaven in a Wild Flower,
Hold Infinity in the palm of your hand,
And Eternity in an hour.

William Blake (1757–1827)

I love all waste
And solitary places;
where we taste
The pleasure of believing
what we see
Is boundless, as we wish
our souls to be.

Percy Bysshe Shelley (1792–1822)

Nature has her music. There is the sound of the wind in the trees, the crashing of waves on the shore, the sweet murmurings of a brook, of cattle in the fields, and sheep on the hillside. Then there are the small sounds of wild animals in the undergrowth. And there is the sound of birdsong.

Some sounds are heard only inside one's head (but they are no less real for that): the warm melody of the sunshine, the sweet harmony of a field of flowers, the singing of the stars.

Since once I sat upon a promontory,
And heard a mermaid on a dolphin's back
Uttering such dulcet and harmonious breath,
That the rude sea grew civil at her song,
And certain stars shot madly from their spheres,
To hear the sea-maid's music.

A Midsummer Night's Dream,
William Shakespeare (1564–1616)

Wherefore philosophers say that we have learned
Our melodies from those of the revolving spheres.
The song of the spheres in their revolutions
Is what men sing with lute and voice.
The faithful hold that the sweet influences of heaven
Can make even harsh voices melodious.
As we are all members of Adam,
We have heard these melodies in Paradise;
Though earth and water have cast their veil upon us,

We retain faint reminiscences of those heavenly songs.
But while we are thus shrouded by gross earthly veils,
How can the tones of the dancing spheres reach us?
Hence it is that listening to music is lovers' food,
Because it recalls to them their primal union with God.
The inward feelings of the mind acquire strength,
Nay, are shown outwardly, under influence of music.

The Spiritual Couplets of Rumi (1207–1273) (Sufi writings)

No voice; but oh!
The silence sank
Like music on my heart.

The Rime of the Ancient Mariner,
Samuel Taylor Coleridge (1772–1834)

How sweet the moonlight sleeps upon this bank!
Here will we sit, and let the sounds of music
Creep in our ears; soft stillness and the night
Become the touches of sweet harmony.

The Merchant of Venice,
William Shakespeare (1564–1616)

Nature brings us rest, serenity, calmness, even in the midst of the bustle of our everyday lives.

When you are in a crowded, noisy city, rushing to an appointment, working, shopping, or simply traveling from one place to another . . . **Stop. Take time. Find nature. Find rest.**

Even in the middle of a city you can find nature. It may be a large formal park, or just a little patch of grass.

Look at the flowers and drink in their beauty. Smell their fragrance. Inhale their life.

Touch a tree. You don't have to hug it. You don't have to feel self-conscious, with others around you. Just touch it. Maybe lean against it, with your hand on its bark. Feel its age. Feel its life. Feel its roots stretching deep into the soil, drinking water, drinking life. Feel its leaves reaching out to the sky, drinking sunlight, drinking life.

Feel at peace. Rest.

If you are in the countryside, and you have climbed a steep hill, and are out of breath . . . stop. Breathe in the fresh air. Smell the sweet, natural scents. Listen to the wind and the birds. See the beauty of God's nature all around you.

Him the wanderer o'er the world
Far away the winds will bear,
And restless care.

Frederick Tennyson (1807–1898), after Sappho (c. 600 B.C.E

From the sound of cool waters heard through
   the green boughs
      Of the fruit-bearing trees,
      And the rustling breeze,
Deep sleep, as a trance, down over me flows.

Frederick Tennyson (1807–1898), after Sappho (c. 600 B.C.E.)

An English home—gray twilight pour'd
On dewy pasture, dewy trees,
Softer than sleep—all things in order stored,
A haunt of ancient peace.

The Palace of Art, Alfred, Lord Tennyson (1809–1892)

Nature also reminds us of the natural cycle of birth and death. In nature, nothing is permanent. Even the shorelines change over the years. Even the mountains alter over the centuries. We need to learn to relax in this impermanence, for it is entirely natural.

The day becomes more solemn and
　　serene
When noon is past—there is a harmony
In autumn, and a lustre in its sky,
Which through the summer is not heard
　　or seen,
As if it could not be, as if it had not been!

Percy Bysshe Shelley (1792–1822)

To every thing there is a season, and a time to every purpose under the heaven:

A time to be born, and a time to die; a time to plant, and a time to pluck up that which is planted;

A time to kill, and a time to heal; a time to break down, and a time to build up;

A time to weep, and a time to laugh; a time to mourn, and a time to dance;

A time to cast away stones, and a time to gather stones together; a time to embrace, and a time to refrain from embracing;

A time to get, and a time to lose; a time to keep, and a time to cast away;

A time to rend, and a time to sew; a time to keep silence, and a time to speak;

A time to love, and a time to hate; a time of war, and a time of peace.

Ecclesiastes 3:1–8

**The following story is an ancient
one from the Sufi tradition.**

I happened to spend the night in a garden with
one of my friends and we found it to be a
pleasant, cheerful place with heart-ravishing
entangled trees; its ground seemed to be paved
with small glass beads whilst, from its vines,
bunches like the Pleiades were suspended.

A garden the water of whose river was limpid
A grove the melody of whose birds was
    harmonious.

The former full of bright-colored tulips,
The latter full of fruits of various kinds;
The wind had in the shade of its trees
Spread out a bed of all kinds of flowers.

The next morning when the intention of returning had prevailed over the opinion of tarrying, I saw that my friend had in his skirt collected roses, sweet basil, hyacinths, and fragrant herbs with the determination to carry them to town; whereon I said: "Thou knowest that the roses of the garden are perishable and the season passes away," and philosophers have said: "Whatever is not of long duration is not to be cherished."

He asked: "Then what is to be done?" I replied: "I may compose for the amusement of those who look and for the instruction of those who are present a book of a Rose Garden, a Gulistan, whose leaves cannot be touched by the tyranny of autumnal blasts and the delight of whose spring the vicissitudes of time will be unable to change into the inconstancy of autumn."

> Of what use will be a dish of roses to thee?
> Take a leaf from my rose-garden.
> A flower endures but five or six days
> But this rose-garden is always delightful.

After I had uttered these words he threw away the flowers from his skirts, and attached himself to mine, saying: "When a generous fellow makes a promise he keeps it."

The Gulistan of Sa'di, Sheik Muslih-Uddin Sa'di Shirazi
(c. 1193–1291) (Sufi writings)

While we enjoy the beauty
of nature, and the rest and
peacefulness it brings to us, we
should also look deeper.
We should look for the
spirituality in nature.

Perhaps you believe that the universe, this world, all of nature, including ourselves, are all part of a natural evolutionary process. You may believe in a personal God, a transcendent Force or Power behind all things, or the immanence of God Within. Either way, there is deep spirituality in nature.

He shall judge thy people with righteousness, and thy poor with judgment.

The mountains shall bring peace to the people, and the little hills, by righteousness.

He shall judge the poor of the people, he shall save the children of the needy, and shall break in pieces the oppressor.

They shall fear thee as long as the sun and moon endure, throughout all generations.

He shall come down like rain upon the mown grass: as showers that water the Earth.

In his days shall the righteous flourish; and abundance of peace so long as the moon endureth. He shall have dominion also from sea to sea, and from the river unto the ends of the Earth.

Psalm 72:2–8

The mountains also shall bring peace
And the little hills righteousness unto
the people.

Psalm 72:3, Book of Common Prayer

peace
and love

In that seemingly never-ending Summer of Love of the late sixties, hippies would often greet each other with "Peace and Love, man." It became a cliché, but the feeling behind it was genuine.

Young people wanted peace, in the world, among themselves, and within each one of them individually; and they realized that the path to peace was through love.

Love is one of the most powerful emotions in human experience. It can often be problematic, even traumatic, yet we all want it. We all want to love and be loved.

Hundreds of thousands of poems and popular songs have been written about love. Think of all the phrases, titles, sayings, and all the proverbs there are about love.

Operas, plays, novels, paintings, sculptures, and great pieces of music have drawn on love for their theme, and for their power to move us. Often, for dramatic tension, they focus on the problems of love, but consider what makes love so attractive to us all.

Think of the love that draws two people together, of any age, race, or gender. Think of the warmth they feel for each other, of the look in their eyes, of the peace in their hearts when they are quietly together.

Oh wind that blows from the sun-rising,
What news of the maid with the drunken eyes,
What news of the lovely maid dost thou bring?
Bid me not wake from my dream and arise,
In dreams I have rested my head at her feet—
When stillness unbroken around me lies,
The vision of her makes my solitude sweet.

Teachings of Hafiz (Sufi writings)

Sleep dwell upon thine eyes,
    peace in thy breast!
Would I were sleep and
    peace, so sweet to rest!

Romeo and Juliet,
William Shakespeare (1564–1616)

And on that cheek, and o'er that brow,
So soft, so calm, yet eloquent,
The smiles that win, the tints that glow
But tell of days in goodness spent,
A mind at peace with all below,
A heart whose love is innocent!

She Walks in Beauty, Lord Byron (1788–1824)

Sure there is music even in the beauty, and the silent note which Cupid strikes, far sweeter than the sound of an instrument. For there is a music wherever there is a harmony, order, or proportion; and thus far we may maintain the music of the spheres; for those well-ordered motions, and regular paces, though they give no sound unto the ear, yet to the understanding they strike a note most full of harmony.

Sir Thomas Browne (1605–1682)

As we all know, the course of true love rarely runs smooth. People who fall in love can also fall out of it, and this is painful to both. The joy and the peace once felt can be lost.

The hope we hold on to is
that we will find love
again, with someone new.

If we are in a loving
relationship, there are
bound to be tensions,
both large and small.
Sometimes, the greater
the problem, the more
determined we both are
to put it right, together.

But the little everyday problems—the niggles, the squabbles—these can cause far more trouble. They can destroy the peace that should be in our hearts when we are in love.

How, then, can we avoid dissension with the one we love? How can we bring peace when our relationship is troubled?

We have to work together to solve our problems. We need to talk—but also to listen. We must forgive, and ask to be forgiven. We have to be honest with each other, and seek peace with each other all the time.

Peace must be at the heart of any loving relationship. If you are at peace with each other, you can relax into your love.

Truly, the Lord loveth union and harmony and abhorreth separation and divorce. Live ye one with another, O people, in radiance and joy. By My life! All that are on earth shall pass away, while good deeds alone shall endure; to the truth of My words God doth Himself bear witness. Compose your differences, O My servants; then heed ye the admonition of Our Pen of Glory and follow not the arrogant and wayward.

Kitáb-i-Aqdas (Bahá'í scriptures)

Well, hasten to comfort her lest her wrath in the end should harden into bitterness. Hasten to fling thine arms about her snowy neck, and press her tear-stained cheek against thy breast. Kiss away her tears, and with her tears mingle the sweet delights of love. Soon she'll grow calm; that is the only way to soothe her wrath. When her rage is at its height, when it is open war between you, then beg her to ratify a peace upon her bed; she'll soon make friends.

'Tis there that, all unarmed, sweet concord dwells; 'tis there, the cradle of forgiveness. The doves that late were fighting, more tenderly will bill and coo; their murmurs seem to tell how true and tender is their love.

The Art of Love, Ovid (43 B.C.E.–C.E. 17)

Comfort is one of the most important aspects of love, whether the special love between two people, or the love between friends. When we comfort each other, we bring peace to each other.

445

To hold someone in your arms
when they are upset—your child,
your partner, your friend—gives
the comfort of physical closeness.
**But more important, it gives
the comfort of knowing
someone cares.**

Often people hide their fears, their pain, their turmoil. Be sensitive to the hidden pain of others. Look, and listen, and feel. And show them you care.

Give your loved ones comfort and peace. Sometimes, friendship in itself is the greatest source of comfort, rest, and repose.

Come to me; what I
  seek in vain
Bring thou; into my
  spirit send
Peace after care, balm
  after pain;
And be my friend.

Frederick Tennyson (1807–1898),
after Sappho (c. 600 B.C.E.)

Oh, the comfort—the inexpressible comfort of feeling safe with a person, having neither to weigh thoughts, nor measure words, but pouring them all out, just as they are, chaff and grain together; knowing that a faithful hand will take and sift them—keep what is worth keeping—and with the breath of kindness blow the rest away.

Friendship, Anonymous

I hold this to be the highest task for a bond between two people: that each protects the solitude of the other.

Rainer Maria Rilke (1875–1926)

Lest Sorrow's army waste thy heart's domain,
I send my life to bring thee peace again,
Dear life thy ransom! From thy singers learn
How one that longs for thee may weep and
    burn
Sonnets and broken words, sweet notes and
    songs
I send to thee.

Teachings of Hafiz (Sufi writings)

When Youth his faery reign began
Ere Sorrow had proclaim'd me man;
While Peace the present hour beguil'd,
And all the lovely Prospect smil'd;
Then Mary! 'mid my lightsome glee
I heav'd the painless Sigh for thee.

The Sigh, Samuel Taylor Coleridge (1772–1834)

The peacefulness we find in nature goes hand in hand with love, whether between two people, within a family, or as the trust and good company of close friends.

There is a wordless promise
in the peace we find in nature,
a promise of perfection, a
remembrance of a Golden
Age, a foretaste of Paradise.

Remember that "**Paradise**"
comes from a Persian word
meaning a park or garden.

Give thanks for nights spent in good company,
And take the gifts a tranquil mind may bring;
No heart is dark when the kind moon doth shine,
And grass-grown riverbanks are fair to see.

Teachings of Hafiz (Sufi writings)

For, lo, the winter is past, the rain is over and gone; the flowers appear on the Earth;

the time of the singing of birds is come, and the voice of the turtle is heard in our land; the fig tree putteth forth her green figs, and the vines with the tender grape give a good smell.

Arise, my love, my fair one, and come away.

Song of Songs 2: 11–13

Acknowledgments

Extracts from the Authorized Version of the bible (The King James Bible), the rights in which are vested in the Crown, are reproduced by permission of the Crown's Patentee, Cambridge University Press.

Extracts from The Book of Common Prayer, the rights of which are vested in the Crown, are reproduced by permission of the Crown's Patentee, Cambridge University Press.

Page 196. Quotation used by permission of the Estate of Robert Service, (c)1921.

Page 208 (top). Quotation used by permission of the Society of Authors, on behalf of the Estate of George Bernard Shaw.

Many thanks to the Baha'i Publishing Trust, UK, for their assistance.

Note: Every effort has been made to trace and contact copyright holders; the publisher would be pleased to hear from any copyright holders not acknowledged.

JAY VICKERS

Jay Vickers has been a teacher of religious studies and English, a computer programmer and intelligence analyst for the British and American governments, and a journalist. Jay has been a full-time freelance writer since 1991, researching and writing mainly on religious and esoteric subjects. Currently researching for a Ph.D. in Sociology of Religion at the University of London, Jay is a frequent speaker on this subject at conferences, and on radio and television.

Under other names, Jay's many books include major studies of new religious movements, and a historical analysis of the beliefs of secret societies.

A regular book critic for numerous newspapers, magazines and websites, Jay Vickers lives in London, England.

Published by MQ Publications Limited
12 The Ivories, 6–8 Northampton Street, London N1 2HY
Tel: 020 7359 2244   Fax: 020 7359 1616

Senior editor: Salima Hirani
Design: Bet Ayer

ISBN: 1–84072–403–X

Printed and bound in China